E Grodzicki
Grodzicki, Jenna.
Baby sea turtles

BABY SEA TURTLES

by Jenna Grodzicki

Consultant: Beth Gambro
Reading Specialist, Yorkville, Illinois

BEARPORT
PUBLISHING

Minneapolis, Minnesota

Teaching Tips

Before Reading

- Look at the cover of the book. Discuss the picture and the title.

- Ask readers to brainstorm a list of what they already know about sea turtles. What can they expect to see in the book?

- Go on a picture walk, looking through the pictures to discuss vocabulary and make predictions about the text.

During Reading

- Read for purpose. Encourage readers to think about sea turtles and the animal life cycle as they are reading.

- If readers encounter an unknown word, ask them to look at the sounds in the word. Then, ask them to look at the rest of the page. Are there any clues to help them understand?

After Reading

- Encourage readers to pick a buddy and reread the book together.

- Ask readers to name three things sea turtles do between the time they hatch and the time they are ready to have babies. Go back and find the pages that tell about these things.

- Ask readers to write or draw something that they learned about sea turtles.

Credits:
Cover, © Petr Jan Juračka / 500px and Getty; © Iakov Kalinin / Shutterstock ; 3, © Noppasin / iStock; 5, © Shakeel Sha / iStock; 5, © Nature Picture Library / Alamy; 6, © Markos Loizou / Shutterstock; 7, © MidoSemsem / Shutterstock; 7, © Noppasin / iStock; 8, © pepifoto / iStock; 9, © Kalaeva / Shutterstock; 11, © Ryan Sutherland / EyeEm / Getty; 13, © Elena Berd / Shutterstock; 15, © Juergen Freund / Alamy; 16–17, © Niyash Nizar / Shutterstock; 18, © Katrin Kaemper / Shutterstock; 19, © hocus-focus / iStock; 20–21, © inhauscreative / iStock; 22, © beltsazar / Shutterstock; 23, © Michael Smith ITWP / Shutterstock; 23, © emirhankaramuk / Shutterstock; 23, © Tommy Daynjer / Shutterstock; 23, © Stephane Bidouze / Shutterstock; 23, © divedog / Shutterstock; 23, © Ohishiapply / Shutterstock.

Library of Congress Cataloging-in-Publication Data

Names: Grodzicki, Jenna, 1979- author.
Title: Baby sea turtles / by Jenna Grodzicki.
Description: Bearcub books. | Minneapolis, Minnesota : Bearport Publishing
   Company, [2022] | Series: Animal babies | Includes bibliographical
   references and index.
Identifiers: LCCN 2021026716 (print) | LCCN 2021026717 (ebook) | ISBN
   9781636913582 (library binding) | ISBN 9781636913650 (paperback) | ISBN
   9781636913728 (ebook)
Subjects: LCSH: Sea turtles--Infancy--Juvenile literature.
Classification: LCC QL666.C536 G76 2022 (print) | LCC QL666.C536 (ebook)
   | DDC 597.92/81392--dc23
LC record available at https://lccn.loc.gov/2021026716
LC ebook record available at https://lccn.loc.gov/2021026717

For more information, write to Bearport Publishing, 5357 Penn Avenue South, Minneapolis, MN 55419. Printed in the United States of America.

Contents

It's a Baby Sea Turtle!

Tap, tap, tap!

A baby sea turtle breaks out of its egg.

It uses its egg tooth to get out.

4

Egg tooth

The baby turtle is called a **hatchling**.

It is smaller than a bar of soap.

The hatchling has a round shell and little **flippers**.

The turtle **hatches** with a lot of other turtles.

It is in a nest by the ocean.

The nest is deep under the sand.

So, the hatchling digs up.

Scratch, scratch!

It may dig for days.

At last, it is free from the sandy nest.

The hatchling waits until night.

Then, it goes to the ocean.

Its flippers help it move across the sand.

Splash!

The hatchling reaches the water.

Now, it uses its flippers to swim.

The baby sea turtle swims for days.

It keeps going until it is far from the **shore**.

The turtle grows up in the ocean.

It floats among **seaweed**.

The young turtle eats **jellyfish** and other small animals.

Yum!

Jellyfish

As years go by, the turtle grows bigger.

Someday, it will swim back to the shore to have babies.

The Baby's Body

Beak

Head

Eye

Shell

Flipper

Tail

Glossary

flippers wide, flat limbs that are used for swimming

hatches comes out of an egg

hatchling a baby turtle

jellyfish an animal that lives in the ocean and has a soft body with long tentacles

seaweed a type of plant that grows in the ocean

shore the land beside the ocean

Index

egg 4
flippers 7, 12, 14, 22
jellyfish 18

nest 8, 10
ocean 8, 12, 18
sand 8, 10, 12
shore 17, 20

Read More

Bassier, Emma. *Sea Turtles (Ocean Animals).* Minneapolis: Abdo Publishing, 2020.

Leaf, Christina. *Sea Turtles (Blastoff! Beginners: Ocean Animals).* Minneapolis: Bellwether Media, 2021.

Learn More Online

1. Go to **www.factsurfer.com** or scan the QR code below.
2. Enter "**Baby Sea Turtles**" into the search box.
3. Click on the cover of this book to see a list of websites.

About the Author

Jenna Grodzicki loves to read and go to the beach with her husband and two children. She once swam with a sea turtle and touched its shell!